Shots for the Soul II

Copyright © 2014 Authored By: Kurt Lykes
All rights reserved.

ISBN: 1493650963
ISBN 13: 9781493650965

Dedication

This book is dedicated in memory of who I would consider to be 'two' of the greatest people to walk on this planet.

My parents,
the epic:

Mr. Willie C. Lykes
and
Mrs. Vivian M. Lykes

I will cherish you forever...

Thank you for teaching me about Jesus, and introducing me to Him.

Because of that,
I will see you again..

Acknowledgements

Though it is virtually impossible for me to list all of the people who have influenced me, and contributed to my journey in order for me to share my thoughts on paper throughout this devotional, I do want to acknowledge you. Thanks to all of you who believed in me, and encouraged me enough to help me see my own value to do this project. Thanks for those who caught the vision, supported it, and prayed throughout the process. Thanks to those who challenged me to come up with a plan and a deadline. Thanks to those who came to my office and made me take time to 'finish what I had started'. Thanks to the team that examined every word, made the adjustments, and patiently walked me through the business side! Whew, what would I do without you! Thanks to my family and friends who listened to my thoughts and provoked me to see God differently. Thanks to my creative team and friends that I called upon for your help, and you took time away from your own projects to help me finish mine! Thanks to all the leaders I've served under, or beside, whether past or present, I've gained so much from serving with you. Thanks to my wife (Mucette), and to my only son (Kaleb Joshua) for your continuous love, support, grace, and acceptance. Most of all, thanks to the Giver of Life and to the One who knows and loves me most, Jesus Christ. It's in You I live, I move, and have my being. You are my everything.

1

'Everyone Needs a Little Grace'

'Be gentle and forbearing with one another and, if one has a complaint against another, be ready to pardon each other, even as the Lord has forgiven you, so must you also forgive.'
-Colossians 3: 12-13

No one is perfect, and all of us need a little grace every now and then.

It can be difficult to forgive at times, but try to consider how God continues to love and forgive us beyond measure.

When we realize how God forgives, and how He pours out His love, it will challenge us to do the same, especially when we 'say' we want to be more and more like Him.

Let's keep in mind that unforgiveness has a greater effect on the one who is carrying it around vs. the offender.

Do yourself a favor... lighten your load, and let it go...

My Thoughts

2

'Stress Free'

'My desire is to have you free from all anxiety and distressing care.'
-1 Corinthians 7:32

God's desire is that you live stress free.

Some of the things we are stressed about are things that 'WE' have brought upon ourselves.

It's time to do something different....
Let's start by making better choices, which will result in lowering the levels of stress.

My Thoughts

3

'GET THE FACTS'

"The end of all things is near. Therefore be clear minded, and self- controlled, so that you can pray."
-1 Peter 4:7

Don't believe everything you hear. Do your research, and check for yourself. Study to show yourselves approved, and get the facts.

People will say things and it will appear to be 'the 'gospel truth', but don't be one that sways with the wind.

Jesus is Lord. Jesus saves. Jesus is the only way.
There are no substitutes, and His truth is sure.

Get control over your thoughts and emotions so that you can have a direct link to the Father when you pray!

Exercise self- control, and don't let situations or others cause you to respond and react in a way that you shouldn't.

Remember, you are the only Jesus that someone may ever see.

My Thoughts

4

'What are You Listening to?'

'..but whoso hearkens to me shall dwell safely and shall be quiet, without fear or dread of evil.'
-Proverbs 1: 33

You can walk in confidence,
feel secure at all times,
have peace of mind,
and have no fear and anxiety,
if you would simply listen to,
and obey the voice of the Lord.

Find a secret place, and listen to what He has to say to you.

Don't make it complicated...
Steal away...and listen.

My Thoughts

5

'Get a Grip'

'Therefore, as God's chosen people, holy and dearly beloved, clothe yourselves with compassion, kindness, humility, gentleness and patience.'
-Colossians 3:12

Remember, you control your responses. No matter what people say or do, you can control how you respond. That is powerful.

Meekness is strength under control. Some people will try to push you to the edge and push your buttons, but as long as you know who you are, and *'whose'* you are, there is no such need to respond.

Treat them with love, compassion, and kindness. Walk in humility and watch God continue to bless you *'right in front of them'!*

He said he would prepare a table before you *IN THE PRESENCE OF* your enemies.
Let them talk...just stay focused, and keep being blessed!

My Thoughts

6

'Practice Makes Perfect'

'...in all of thy ways acknowledge Him and
He will direct your path.'
-Proverbs 3:6

Before you make any decisions, acknowledge God.... ask for direction, ask for wisdom, ask for guidance, ask for peace, and don't forget to ask for His will to be done.

Once you acknowledge Him, you can rest assured that as you move forward, He is with you, and will direct you along the way.

It's a promise.

Practice makes perfect, so continue to practice acknowledging Him first, in ALL things, and see how different life will be!

My Thoughts

7

'Speak Up'

"Trust in Him at all times, you people; pour out your hearts to Him, for God is our refuge."
-Psalms 62:8

You can never talk too much to God!
He is ALWAYS listening, and ALWAYS ready to hear from us!

He desires that we would bring everything to Him in prayer..*FIRST,* not after we've already tried every way to figure it out and failed.

Trust that He has the answer to all of our concerns, and as we come to Him, He will give us our daily bread, and direction for each new day.

There is safety and comfort in His presence, and He is more concerned about the cares of your heart than you could ever imagine.

If you haven't gone to Him today, and poured out your heart, STOP, and do it right now..He's waiting..

My Thoughts

8

'A Path to Peace'

"Blessed are the peacemakers, for they will be called the children of God."
-Matthew 5:9

Do you know one of the *BEST* ways to keep peace?

Keep your mouth closed!

It is said, that is why we have two eyes, two ears, and *ONE* mouth.

God's promise is that you will be blessed when you seek to create an atmosphere of peace.

Remember when Jesus simply knelt down, wrote in the sand, but had nothing verbally to say?

His mere silence spoke volumes to the need for that situation.

WE CAN DO THE SAME! Be a peacemaker...

My Thoughts

9

'STAY TUNED IN'

'Do nothing out of selfish ambition or vain conceit, but in humility consider others better than yourselves. Each of you should look not only to your own interests, but also to the interests of others.'
-Philippians 2: 3-4

Be careful not to always make everything about you...

When someone is talking, don't be so quick to jump in and share how 'you' feel or how 'you've' been through something similar.

You may have better skills or more experiences than others around you, but you don't have to broadcast it and let them and everyone else know.

Pride is subtle, and it seeks to destroy us all. Watch out for it, and seek after humility. You'd be surprised to see how much you could learn by being interested in what 'others' have to share!

My Thoughts

10

'It's in You'

"As you go, proclaim this message: The kingdom of God has come near.."
-Matthew 10:7

Remember that everywhere you go, God is there, with you and in you.

THE KINGDOM OF GOD IS WITHIN YOU!

You are the only part of Jesus that someone may ever see...

You are called to pray for the sick, the hurting, the broken, the poor, the needy...and the list goes on and on.

Be the Jesus that others need to see.

When you come into contact with anyone, know that literally, for them.. the Kingdom of God has come near, because of you...

My Thoughts

11

'Lifetime Guarantee'

'...his favor lasts a lifetime..'
-Psalms 30:5

God has been good, and His favor is on your life!
As His child, you have everything you need for the journey.. and then some!

Do not 'downplay' God's blessings!
If He has been good to you, talk about it!

Even with all of the changes with the 'economy',
God is *STILL* releasing favor and blessings!
Someone may need to hear that God is still moving, simply by you sharing with them about His favor!

That doesn't give you a license to be arrogant... but it does give you liberty to tell what He has done, and all that He is doing in your life!

You have favor because HE gives it to you, and not just for a season, but for a **LIFETIME!**

Be proud of your heavenly Father today, and thank Him for His favor!
He's been GOOD!

My Thoughts

12

'Who's Judging?'

"It is God who judges; He brings down one, He exalts another."
-Psalms 75:7

Be very careful with your words.
Don't be so quick to put your opinion on everything!
Remember, you have more than enough that you could
be tending to concerning your own life.

It is God who chooses to exalt and abase.

You may want to 'get your thoughts out', but at the end of the day...

<u>'WHERE THERE IS NO RESPONSIBILITY,
THERE SHOULD BE NO OPINION."</u>

My Thoughts

13

'DON'T TELL IT ALL'

"..but he who holds his tongue is wise."
-Proverbs 10:19

Everybody doesn't need to know everything! ..and no one needs to know *ALL* of your business.

Try not to overdo it and 'over-share'.
Instead, try to become a better listener by asking questions and getting more understanding.

You don't always have to be the one 'being heard'.

Exercise wisdom, and learn to tame that tongue..

My Thoughts

14

'Attitude Adjustment'

*"Because Your love is better than life, my lips will glorify You.
I will praise You as long as I live.. and in Your name
I will lift up my hands."*
-Psalm 63:3-4

NO MATTER WHAT... keep an attitude of gratitude!

HE will bring you through!!

Giving up and letting go is **NOT** an option...

Keep your head up, and keep that attitude in check!

Cancel out the thoughts and noises of negativity!

Choose to believe the best, and keep the praises ringing..

GOD is in control..

HE WILL NOT LET YOU GO!

My Thoughts

15

'Never Alone'

"...and I am with you always, even until the end of the world."
-Matthew 28:20

If you ever question in the back of your mind whether God is with you or not, here's a precious promise!

Sometimes it may 'feel' that God isn't listening, that He is busy helping others and has forgotten all about you. You may feel alone and things could seem unbearable.. BUT---HE IS 'ALWAYS' WITH YOU!

Take courage in knowing that HE is there.
There is a reason for this very test you're going through, and the season that you're in. God has a plan.. so take courage and hold on!

HE IS WITH YOU child of God!

My Thoughts

16

'Think for a Change'

"Finally brothers, whatever is true, whatever is noble, whatever is right, whatever is pure, whatever is lovely, whatever is admirable- if anything is excellent or praiseworthy, --think about such things."
-Philippians 4:8

The mind will always try to tell you what to do, how to react, and how to think..

More than half of the battle is mental, so you have to control and guard your thoughts! Stop thinking about *'THAT THING'* so much, and replace it with something else.

Replace negative thoughts with positive ones. Replace fear and worry with hope and possibility! Think of all God's already done for you. He is **NOT** going to let you fail!

This can be challenging, and if wishing problems away worked all of the time, life would be rather easy. However, even if they don't go away, dare to imagine your circumstance working in your favor. Imagine the outcome being one that will make you better, make you smarter, or teach you a lesson that you didn't know before you experienced it.

It's easy to believe the worst, but just think how great your life could be when you see *'everything'* as an opportunity for you to grow. Changing your perspective could be just what you need right now..

My Thoughts

17

'Seek and Ye Shall Find'

"Those who know Your name will trust in You, For You, Lord, have never forsaken those who seek You.."
-Psalm 9:10 (NIV)

Keep trusting God... He has what you need.

Keep calling on His name.. He hears you, and is much closer than you know.

He will NOT let you drown! It may be tough, but you can handle it!

Trust Him, and keep doing what you know to do!

He will do the rest...

My Thoughts

18

'A Gift Worth Receiving'

"For by grace you have been saved, through faith and that not of yourselves; it is the gift of God."
-Ephesians 2:8 (NKJV)

Don't ever try to earn your salvation, or get God's attention through your 'good behavior'.

God's love is a gift!
God's grace is a gift!
Salvation is His gift to us!

Although we should strive to do our best to live right and to do good, our goodness could never merit His favor or His love!

Thank Him today that He loves us just the way we are... and will love us 'into' all that we will ever be!

My Thoughts

19

'Write Life in Pencil'

"In his heart a man plans his course, but the Lord determines His steps."
-Proverbs 16:9 (NIV)

A wise man once told me: "Write life in pencil, because things are always subject to change."

Just wanted to remind you this week that although you may have your life all mapped out, make sure to leave room for God's plan!

At any moment, He can flip the script, and we all need to be ok with that!

Don't be discouraged if things didn't work out the way you imagined it would, because God knows exactly what you need, and makes no mistakes!

Your steps are ordered!

My Thoughts

20

'Expectations'

"It is better to trust in the Lord, than to put confidence in men.'
-Psalms 118:8

This speaks for itself..
It is loud and clear.
So ask yourself: "What have I been expecting from 'man',
that I should be expecting from God?"

Be honest.. take inventory..
This shot can be quite sobering...

My Thoughts

21

'Finish Strong'

"..Being confident in this very thing, that He who began a good work in you will complete it.."
-Philippians 1:6

HE will finish what HE started in you!
Do your part, and HE will do the rest.

Don't quit, and don't look backwards!
Don't keep thinking about all you've lost,
think about all there is to gain, and what is in front of you!

Your best days are still yet to be seen!
History is always being made, and records are forever being broken..
So why not you...?
Leaders aren't made overnight..
they are built over a lifetime! Stay focused!

My Thoughts

22

'HE CARRIES YOUR LOAD'

"Casting the whole of your care (all your anxieties, all your worries, all your concerns, once and for all) on Him, for He cares for you affectionately and cares about you watchfully."
-1 Peter 5:7

Do you not know that everything that concerns you concerns God?
He is watching over you daily, and surrounding you with His presence.

Even when you can't see Him, He is there..
When you can't feel Him, He is there..
When you doubt and feel all alone, He is still there...

Although there are aspects in this life that will bring disaster, hurt, financial hardship, broken promises, setbacks, and lots of pain, God desires to bring us through **ALL** of them, and to make us stronger as we walk *'thru'* the fire WITH HIM!

He is closer than you know! When you start to feel overwhelmed with the cares of the day, simply stop and pray and say to God:
'I'm casting this on You Lord.. I know you can handle it much better than I can..'

Hear His reply: 'I am with you my child, even until the end of the world..'

My Thoughts

23

'Check the Thermometer'

*"A hot-tempered man stirs up dissension,
but a patient man calms a quarrel."*
-Proverbs 15:18

Learn to control your temper. Everyone has one,
and no matter how saved you are, or 'think' you are,
your attitude can flare up at any time!

Exercise self- control and discipline over your attitude.
This is not easy, but patience is a fruit of the spirit.

Learning to hold your tongue at the right moment, at the right time,
in the right place, could be the very thing that saves a meaningful
relationship! Think about it....

<u>*'Most' of the time' ---the thing that you'd like
to say about or to that person....they already know! LOL!!!*</u>

Be patient, and keep that temper under control!

My Thoughts

24

'Lace up Your Shoes'

*"For You are my hiding place; You protect me from trouble.
You surround me with songs of victory."*
-Psalm 32:7

Where do you run when the cares of life wear you down?
Where do you go to find peace in the midst of adversity?
There is a place to run that is safe for the believer..

RUN TO GOD!

In Him, you will find ALL that you need. He will protect your heart when the world wants to step on it. He will comfort you, when others are laughing at you. He will hold you when friends let go. He will stand with you when family has walked away..
He is there, and will always be there..

RUN TO GOD...

If you are still and quiet enough, you may even hear Him sing to you..

RUN TO GOD!

My Thoughts

25

'New Season'

"Behold, I make ALL things new.."
-Revelation 21:5

Things are beginning to shift..
Feel and sense the newness God is bringing into your surroundings..

It is time!
Expect..Expect..Expect..
God is up to GOOD concerning you!

He is doing a 'new' thing in you.
Brace yourself for the journey..it is good!

Don't think about what you may have to let go of...

Think of ALL the things that await your arrival!

Get ready... you're making history!

My Thoughts

26

'The Waiting Room'

"I waited patiently and expectantly for the Lord; and He inclined to me and heard my cry."
-Psalm 40:1

What have you been crying out to God about?

Whatever it is, know that He hears you, and in due time He will answer.

Acquiring patience is one of life's lessons that is an on-going process.

Having the right attitude while acquiring patience is also an important factor while in the process.

Learning to have the proper attitude and perspective about our situations, and still expecting things to get better, <u>*can only be accomplished*</u> <u>*as we look to God!*</u>

It takes God's strength, and His help...so don't be afraid to ask Him for it! His desire is to grow us into ALL we are supposed to be, to give us ALL we're supposed to have, and to work in us His perfect plan for our lives!

As you set out to seek Him, Ask Him to help you with your attitude.

Wait patiently as He develops you into the person you were created to be!

It's an exciting ride, so brace up, and enjoy the journey!

My Thoughts

27

'It's That Time

"So shall you find favor, good understanding, and high esteem in the sight of God and man."
-Proverbs 3:4

Prepare yourself for God's favor!

Start noticing that the winds are shifting around you for good!
It is time for you to be blessed!

Your endurance, and your faithfulness is now ready to be rewarded!

Look for it.. expect it.. in everything.. NO LIMITS..
and thank God EVERY time it happens.. whether large or small.
It is time...

Look for good things to come into your life..

My Thoughts

28

'BE HIS SHADOW'

"The LORD is gracious, and full of compassion;
slow to anger, and of great mercy."
-Psalm 145:8

The Lord is gracious, so we should strive to be..

He is full of compassion...are you compassionate?

He is SLOW to anger.. need I ask?

..and He shows great mercy. Do you?

We could read this and simply say: 'Thank God that He is not like me, because I'm human, and I don't understand how He does it, but thank God for Jesus."

Or we could say: 'Lord, I want to look more like You, and have Your heart. Show me how to be an example of Your grace. Teach me compassion for Your people. Help me to control my attitude and keep my emotions under control. Make me Your vessel of mercy!"

Which one sounds like you?

My Thoughts

29

'Give it Your All'

"Whatever you do, work at it with all your heart, as working for the Lord, not for men."
-Colossians 3:23, (NIV)

Remember, God is the one who rewards you at the end of the day.

Don't do just enough to get by.
Don't be average.
Whenever you commit to doing anything, do it with all of your heart!

God is watching to see if you will be faithful!

He remembers when others forget!

You may feel that you are *'always'* the one doing, giving,
sacrificing, forgiving, holding your tongue, bending, compromising,
serving, and patiently waiting....

Just remember that **GREAT** is your reward
when you expect it from GOD, and not from men.

Whatever you do, great or small.. do it with ALL of your heart,
as working for the Lord, not for men.

He will bless you.. stay focused!

My Thoughts

30

'Count Your Blessings'

"O give thanks to the Lord, for He is good; for His mercy and loving-kindness endures forever!"
-1 Chronicles 16:34, (AMP)

We have MUCH to be thankful for..

Count your blessings..

Thank God that things are as good as they are.

Yes, you may have had a few setbacks this year,
but each day you wake up, it presents another
opportunity for things to change!

That's the kind of God we serve! *Miracles still happen!*
He can change your situation in the blink of an eye!

Expect God to move, and He will.

When you can give thanks in the midst of it all,
it is a testament to how you trust in, and know your Father!

My Thoughts

31

'WHAT ARE YOU DOING?

'So you see, faith by itself isn't enough.'
-James 2:17

Simple word today:

Are you *'doing'* or are you just *'hoping and thinking'*?

Faith alone isn't enough.

My Thoughts

32

'It all Belongs to Him'

"The earth is the LORD'S, and everything in it, the world, and ALL who live in it."
-Psalms 24:1

If there is a need, God can meet it.
If there is a problem, God can handle it.
If there is a concern, God sees and He cares...

Everything belongs to God.. everything!
and if you need it, He has it..

Our time isn't His time, and although you may feel that time is running out, remember- God's timing is perfect!

He never makes a mistake, and He knows just what you need.

The EARTH and everything in it 'belongs to Him'..

He WILL provide!

My Thoughts

33

'Fight the Right War'

"For our struggle is not against flesh and blood, but against the rulers, against the powers, and against the world forces of this darkness, against the spiritual forces of wickedness in the heavenly places."
-Ephesians 6:12

We have a fight to fight at **ALL** times, but that fight isn't against flesh and blood.
Behind every thing that makes your blood levels rise, and would make you want to *'throw down'*, is a spiritual force thwarted to throw you off track!

When situations arise as such, we must remember to take a step back, breathe, and know who and what it is we are fighting! We have an enemy who does **NOT** want us to walk in victory, *or see ANY parts of it!*

You can be having the greatest day, and 'WHAM'.. out of nowhere, a simple conversation, a phone call, a facial gesture, or even a thought, could set you off and send you on the path of war!

BE AWARE that the enemy is out to steal your joy at ALL times, and again, it is not the people or things that are targeting you, but it <u>*IS the enemy 'USING' those people and things to do it!*</u>

Fight the right opponent, or you are fighting the wrong war!

My Thoughts

34

'Work on You'

"Do not judge or you too will be judged.."
-Matthew 7:1

Simple as that:

Stop judging or you too will be judged..

We **ALL** need grace, and we **ALL** need love..

Work on what 'you' need to work on,
and pray that others might do the same..

My Thoughts

35

'Giant Killer'

"Have I not commanded you? Be strong and courageous. Do not be afraid; do not be discouraged, for the Lord your God will be with you wherever you go."
-Joshua 1:9

It takes faith to follow God!
It takes courage to step out and do what He's called you to do.

Sometimes the opposition is so fierce that you may begin to question whether or not what you're pursuing is from God, but always know that when God gives you the vision, all hell will break loose when you start moving in the direction of following His call!

The forces or darkness will try to squash, kill, be-little, and thwart your progress, but **MOVE FORWARD** despite it all!

Giants didn't stop Joshua, and neither should any 'giants' stop you! Follow that dream, and know that God is there to hold your hand through the valleys and rough patches!

He says: *'I AM WITH YOU'!*

Don't fear! Be bold! That's what it takes to be a giant killer!

My Thoughts

36

'Refreshments'

'Those who refresh others, will themselves be refreshed.'
-Proverbs 11:25

A little encouragement goes a long way.

You'd be surprised how your little acts of kindness have touched another person's life.
They may never tell you, and you may sometimes feel that
what you say and do goes unnoticed, but it doesn't.

The truth is: **GOD** sees... and that's what matters most.

BE a blessing, BE an encouragement, BE positive, and see how it comes right back to you...just when you need it the most!

Today, refresh someone's life with some positive words or an act of love.

My Thoughts

37

'It's all Good'

> *"A man's mind plans his way, but the Lord directs his steps and makes them sure."*
> -Proverbs 16:9, (AMP)

Life does not always turn out the way
you planned or wished it could be.

Many of us grow up 'dreaming' in our hearts of what our lives would
be like when we turned a certain age...oh well! Lol!

We must remember that although it is a great thing to plan, it is even greater
to *'write life in pencil'*! EVERYTHING is subject to change..at any moment..

Our steps are ordered by the Lord, and we've got to learn to 'trust'
Him for every step of the way. The things, the situations, the people,
the victories, and even the rough patches, are all a part of His plan.

We may not always like it, or even agree, but God's heart is for us,
not against us, and if He has allowed it to be, it is a good thing.

Tell yourself this today..

'God, I trust that You have allowed _____ to come into my life for a
purpose and for Your ultimate will. At times, I don't like it, and I may not
understand why You've allowed it, but I believe that in the end it will give
You glory, so I choose to see this as good...

Thank You for Your strength to help me endure.. 'In Jesus' name, Amen

My Thoughts

38

'God will Fight for You'

"When he was accused by the chief priests and the elders, he gave no answer. Then Pilate asked him, 'Don't you hear the testimony they are bringing against you?' But Jesus made no reply, not even to a single charge — to the great amazement of the governor."
-Matthew 27:12–14, (NIV)

Let God fight for you! Don't spend time trying to defend yourself, and the things that you know to be true.

This is an awesome lesson we can learn from Jesus,
knowing how to tame your tongue and your temper.
He exercised 'great' discipline, in the face of accusation!

You will have critics, accusers, and doubters when it
comes to the dreams that are in your heart, but that comes with
the territory!

You will even have those who testify falsely against you,
or even take words that you've spoken, and twist them..

Whatever the case, stay focused, and don't fight in your own strength,
.... allow God to fight for you!

It will amaze people when you put into practice the discipline of
a 'tamed' tongue, and a 'controlled' temper.

My Thoughts

39

'UPSIDE DOWN'

*"This is the day that the Lord has made,
I will rejoice and be glad in it.."*
-Proverbs 118:24

There are **MANY** things to be grateful for today!
Of course there are setbacks and challenges that we face daily, but <u>perspective</u> is everything!

Look for the good in the midst of the bad..

Instead of saying.. 'It's early, and I didn't get enough sleep,'
say: 'Thank God that I woke up this morning!'

Instead of saying.. 'These gas prices are way too high,'
say: 'Thank You Lord that I have a car to drive around in!'

Instead of saying.. 'I got to get up and go to this job, and work with these crazy people',
say: 'Thank God that I have a job to go to, and that I will get paid for my hard work!'

Things could always be a lot worse, and we tend to only recognize what we have been blessed with once it's gone!

Choose to be *positive!*

Choose to be *grateful*!

Stop complaining and murmuring, and rejoice ***TODAY!***

My Thoughts

40

'STAY IN YOUR LANE'

'Therefore brethren, stand fast, and hold the traditions which you have been taught..'
-2 Thessalonians 2:15

Hold on to what God has shown 'you'.
Everyone is different, and no one can do what God has created 'you' to do.

If you're not careful, when things don't add up the way 'you' think they should, it is easy to listen to other's advice and try to get results another way.

This could possibly cause you to get off track and take even longer to fulfill what 'you' are supposed to be doing. Don't get distracted!

No matter how long it takes, stay the course, and stay in 'your' lane! Although everything around you may be changing, doesn't mean that you have to!

Stay focused, and keep listening to God's direction for 'your' life!

My Thoughts

41

'NO ALTERNATIVES'

"..but the people who know their God shall prove themselves strong and shall stand firm and do exploits {for God}."
-Daniel 11:32

Every setback is a set-up for a comeback!
If you've been walking with the Lord for any length of time, you probably understand exactly what that means.

When you really 'know' God, and have an intimate relationship with Him, you may not always agree with His methods that form you into what He's purposed in His heart for you to be, but somehow you 'know' that ultimately what He is doing in and through you will bring Him glory!

In times like these, our job is to keep standing.. knowing that there is no alternative for those who 'know' Him!

Keep standing! Don't waiver.. you 'know' what He's told you! Stand firm! It's just a matter of time..

My Thoughts

42

'THINK LIKE JESUS'

"Let this mind be in you, which is also in Christ Jesus."
-Philippians 2:5

What's on your mind, and occupying your thoughts today?

What are you thinking about? Failure or victory?

Do you have a mindset that you are the 'victor' or the 'victim'?

Do you try to make peace or stir up confusion?

Do you tend to run off at the mouth, or know when to stay quiet?

Are you confident or do you struggle with insecurity?

Are you a giver or a taker?

Are you one who seeks to be a blessing, or one who is looking for the 'hook up'?

Do you genuinely care about those who are lost, or could you care less?

Are you about kingdom business, or are you too busy concerned about your own?

These are just a few questions to get you 'thinking'....so...what's on your mind today?

Let this mind be in you, which is also in Christ Jesus..

My Thoughts

43

'Share Your Faith'

"Everyone who acknowledges me publicly here on earth, I will also acknowledge before my Father in heaven."
-Matthew 10:32

Do NOT be afraid to share your faith with others. Do NOT be ashamed to acknowledge who you belong to.

We are given many opportunities on a daily basis to share Christ's love with someone, and we must always try to take advantage of those precious moments.

Some political parties say that it is offensive to share your beliefs with others, but at the end of the day, you could be the very one who helps rescue a lost soul, and bring them to Jesus.

Today, purposely look for an opportunity to share Christ with someone.

My Thoughts

44

'IT'

"For there is a proper time and procedure for every matter.."
-Ecclesiastes 8:6 (NIV)

Things take time..

"**It**" will happen when it's time for "**it**" to happen.

Your "**it**" will take time, so relax, and simply give "**it**" a little more time.

"**It**" will come together.. wait for "**it**".

"**It**" is all in God's timing.

What is your "it"?

Remember, God will bring "it" to pass!

My Thoughts

45

'Help is on the Way'

*"Don't be afraid, for I am with you.
Don't be discouraged, for I am your God.
I will strengthen you and help you.
I will hold you up with my victorious right hand."*
-Isaiah 41:10

There is no need to fear. Do not let fear get the upper hand. Do not give into the fear. Move forward, God is with you.

Stop re-living the past. There is nothing you can do about it now, but learn from it, and make better decisions when the opportunities arise to do so. Move forward, God is with you.

Although what has happened to you may have hurt, and although you may still be shedding tears, know that it is ok, for God will give you *strength* during this time, and help you get through it.

He is holding you in His loving hand, and you already have the victory! Again, don't be afraid.. He is your helper.

My Thoughts

46

'BE CONTENT'

"..for I have learned how to be content with whatever I have."
-Philippians 4:11

Be content with where you are, with what you have,
and with whom God has placed in your life...

<u>Things could always be worse.</u>

Many times we wish things could be different, and that
things could change, but consider.. there is another alternative...

<u>Things don't have to be as good as they are.</u>

Instead of murmuring and complaining, grumbling and
and asking 'why me'?? -give thanks for things being as well as they are...

Thank God for the simple things, and keep trusting and
believing that He makes ALL things beautiful....*in His time!*

For now, be *'CONTENT'*, and do your best to keep giving thanks!

My Thoughts

47

'LEAN ON HIM'

"It is better to trust in the Lord, than to put confidence in man."
-Psalms 118:8

God's love never changes. When He promises something, it will happen!
He is consistent, and has promised to be there whenever we need Him.

Your heart can be trusted in His hands, because He won't break it.
Your plans and dreams will flourish when you involve Him in them.
Your life will only get better, when you trust His direction and advice.

He is more than enough.....He is everything!

If you are finally getting tired, it's probably time to lean on Him...

My Thoughts

48

'There is a Plan'

*"For I know the plans I have for you, "says the Lord."
They are plans for good and not for disaster, to give you
a future and a hope."*
-Jeremiah 29:11

God has a plan for your life. There is a very good reason that things are the way they are right now. He knows the reason, and He knows exactly how long you will be in this place..

Remember, there is a strategy and a plan for you to be right where you are, at this time, in this place, and it is God who has divinely placed you here.

This thing will not destroy you. Although you feel the weight of it, you have been developing spiritual muscles all along to endure and carry this load.

You are not alone, and when the time comes for help to arise, God will provide.

It's all a part of a bigger picture, and a plan that will give Him glory, give you the victory, and bless someone else.

Only wait, and don't worry.. His plan is good..

My Thoughts

49

'How High can You Fly?'

"Your attitude should be the same as that of Christ Jesus.."
-Philippians 2:5

What challenge or situation are you facing today where this applies most?

Remember, your attitude will determine your altitude!

Stay focused!

How is your attitude today?

What are you going to do about it?

My Thoughts

50

'GOD HAS THE FINAL WORD'

"The wicked plot against the godly; they snarl at them in defiance. But the Lord just laughs, for He sees their day of judgment coming.."
-Psalm 37:12-13

We've all heard the saying: "I'll get the last laugh".
Well this is what God says to your enemies!

Those who have plotted against you, who are out to get you, <u>*will have their day*</u>..
They may take advantage of you now, and may feel that
they've gotten the best of you, <u>**but they won't get away with it forever.**</u> Their day is coming... says the Lord!

It may 'feel' unfair to be the recipient of the evil schemes that individuals practice, <u>**but God sees it all, and will not let their actions go unnoticed.**</u>

It's amazing that He's laughing, when we're usually crying! This is because He knows the end of the story! **WE WIN..!!**

Remember, in this life we will have MANY tribulations, but in the end..
WE WIN!!!

Let them snarl at you, laugh at you, and rejoice in their ignorance.
God is not mocked, and He is not a man who lies...He will repay!
He has the last laugh!

My Thoughts

51

'It's Just a Test'

*"For He knows the way I take; when He has tested me,
I will come forth as gold."*
-Job 23:10

When times are difficult, it's easy to ask the question, *"Why?"*

We must simply remember that God uses **'nouns'**- (persons, places, and things) to get us to a place called- 'growth'.

Everything He purposes and allows to happen in our lives is used to mature us, grow us up, and make us the men and women we need to be for His ultimate purpose and plan.

We must also remember that there is nothing new under the sun, and what we're facing right now is not new!

Someone else has already been through, and come through what we may be currently facing.

Hold on, and don't throw in the towel!
He knows how much you can bear, and He has promised that you don't have to do it alone! This is only a test...

My Thoughts

52

'LISTEN WITHOUT BEING EXTRA'

"Understand this, my dear brothers and sisters: You must all be quick to listen, slow to speak.."
-James 1:19

Everyone loves having a good listener in their life. When someone intently gives you their undivided attention, and doesn't add their comments or advice every few seconds, their company is always welcomed.

Are you a good listener? Do you listen with the intent to understand, or are you the person who can't wait to respond, anticipating the moment to give your opinion or resolve to the matter at hand?

When someone comes to you to talk, remember that unless they are asking you for your input or advice, they may simply be venting, and needing a listening ear. They may not need an answer or direction, they may just want to verbalize how 'they' are feeling.

The bible says: 'Be quick to listen, and **SLOW** to speak'. This takes much practice and discipline. *(Especially if you're an over-opinionated individual)*

Remember, there's a reason God made us with 2 ears, and 1 mouth... Practice being a better listener, and watch how much of a blessing you can be..

My Thoughts

53

'PAYBACK'

"The foolish shall not stand in Thy sight, Thou hatest all workers of iniquity.."
-Psalm 5:5

Those who do you wrong will pay.
Remember, Vengeance is the Lord's..

You just keep walking upright, and no matter how much you may 'want' to, DO NOT repay evil for evil!

God WILL take care of you! Be strong and do what's right!

My Thoughts

54

'A Helping Hand'

"Carry each other's burdens, and in this way you will fulfill the law of Christ."
-Galatians 6:2 NIV

Everyone could use a helping hand.

Your helping hand could be the very one that makes someone else's day.

All of us face challenges daily, whether great or small,
but having someone say or do something that is encouraging always helps.

Look to be a blessing! Look to lift someone's spirit...
Say a kind word... build someone up....
Pray with someone... or offer a listening ear..

When you do this, you are lifting a burden off of someone's shoulder, and fulfilling the law of Christ!

In short, you put a smile on God's face!☺

My Thoughts

55

'IT WILL GET BETTER'

*"The LORD hath been mindful of us:
He will bless us..."*
-Psalm 115:12

EVERYTHING you are experiencing right now is for a divine reason...
You will come out of this better, and blessed!

Of course *'if you'* were in control, you would change it all...
but not so with God.. His plan is better, and you **WILL** be blessed!

Continue to 'endure'...at all costs!
It may be tough right now, but *'YOU CAN DO IT'*!

It may be taking a while for things to come together,
but <u>KEEP moving forward!</u> **HE IS MINDFUL OF YOU,
HE SEES WHAT YOU'VE BEEN ENDURING,** *and its only*
<u>a matter of time that things WILL change!</u>

Hold on child of God, it will get better..

My Thoughts

56

'LIVE TO GIVE'

"One person gives freely, yet gains even more; another withholds unduly, but comes to poverty."
-Proverbs 11:24

Learn to live to give. There is not much more that fulfills the heart than when we give.

It is amazing how the Lord continues to multiply the little that you 'feel' you have and somehow the cup never runs out. Why? Because you are giving...

This principle works! I have seen it operate in my own life, and I'm sure that many of you have also!

Just because the economy has changed doesn't mean that we must decrease in our giving. Although the world says that now is the time to hold on to the little you have, we operate by a different standard! We live to give, trusting God to keep His promise and supply us with more.

I have seen and heard individuals who have intended to save money, cut back on spending, and withheld being a blessing to others, complain about why it seems their situation goes from bad to worse! Don't allow yourself to fall into that trap!

God's word is truth and life, and speaks for itself!
Give, and give, and give! Find different ways to give! Be creative with your giving, and continue to trust God to give back to you more than you can imagine!

My Thoughts

57

'Teammates'

"Unless the Lord builds the house, its builders labor in vain."
-Psalm 127:1

Remember you and God are a team. We must depend upon God to do for us what we cannot do for ourselves, but we must also to the same degree depend on Him to 'enable us' to do what we must do for ourselves.

God is ALL powerful. and He can do whatever He wants.
On earth, we are His hands and feet, and He uses us as His instruments to fulfill His purpose.

Many times we do things without inquiring His direction, and when it doesn't succeed, we feel God hasn't come through for us. Then there are times we wait for Him to do things for us but we have made no efforts to partner up with Him and do our part.

Simply recognize that you and God are a team, and He desires that you WIN in every area of your life! Start playing like you have a teammate, and see the tables turn!

My Thoughts

58

'Hold Things Loosely'

"Naked I came from my mother's womb, and naked I will depart. The Lord gave and the Lord has taken away, may the name of the Lord still be praised."
-Job 1:20-21

No matter how hard we try, it is NOT up to us what comes and goes in our lives. God is sovereign...

That's why it is important for us to embrace and enjoy every blessing while we can, and live in the moment. Nothing is guaranteed to last forever...

We shouldn't ever have a mentality which causes us to believe that we 'deserve' what we have, or that we are entitled to anything.

Life itself is a gift from God, and He knows what we need, and what we can handle.

We must learn to hold on 'loosely' to the treasures of this world, because this is not our home.. for in this life, things will come and go.

We must always remember that every blessing God gives us to enjoy is temporary, in comparison to eternity!

No matter what comes or goes, we must declare as Job did.. STILL I WILL PRAISE HIM!

I came in here with nothing, and I will leave here with nothing! He is in absolute control, and I thank Him for allowing me to experience all that I have along the way...GOD be praised!

My Thoughts

59

'CAN YOU ENDURE?'

*'But he knows the way I take; when he has tested me,
I will come forth as gold.'*
-Job 23:10

The Lord not only knows the way you take, but He has ordered your steps. He is guiding you and leading you gently by His powerful hand.

He is *growing you, maturing you, and making you into 'ALL' He created you to be.*

This is only a test... a test of your endurance!

Can you endure? Can you hold on? Can you finish well?

Sure you can, because your 'COACH' is doing every exercise along side with you!

WITH God, all things are possible! This is only a test!

My Thoughts

60

'Making a Way'

*"..but forget all of that.. it is nothing compared to what I am going to do. For I am about to do something new.
See I have already begun! Do you not see it?
I will make a pathway through the wilderness.
I will create rivers in the dry wasteland.
-Isaiah 43:18-19*

What you are about to step into is beyond anything you've ever seen or done! It is absolutely new! You've never seen it happen this way before. <u>**This is a new season**</u>.

For those who have ears to ear, hear what God is saying.
<u>**It is now time to move forward.**</u>

He is opening doors that were once shut, and making a way for you. He is removing those things that once held you bound to step out and move forward. <u>**Now is the time... move forward.**</u>

The favor is on you now.. don't delay. Trust God to move before you as you pursue your promise!

It doesn't matter how many times it hasn't worked before. The lessons you were supposed to learn were learned, <u>**and now is the time to move forward!**</u>

<u>*Good things are coming your way...great things are in store.. get ready!*</u>

God is up to good concerning you.. **MOVE FORWARD!**

My Thoughts

61

'BE THANKFUL…NOW!'

"We do not know what a day may bring forth.."
-Proverbs 27:1

Live life today! Forget about the problems.. don't worry, don't stress.
Enjoy the now! Make the best out of 'this' day!
Do something that brings joy to you!

You don't know from moment to moment what is going to happen.
One phone call could change your life forever.
It could be good.. or it could be not so pleasant.

Think about all of the things you can be thankful for 'NOW'.
Think about the good times, the happy times, the fun moments…

Laugh out loud. Laugh hard..
This could even be the day that favor overwhelms you..
It could be the day that you see change happen the way you've dreamed of!

Live in the moment.
…this could be your day!

My Thoughts

62

'Be Ready'

*"He does as He pleases among the angels of heaven,
and among the people of the earth.
NO ONE can stop Him or say to Him,
What do you mean by doing these things?"*
-Daniel 4:35

God is sovereign, and if you haven't come to grips with that, ..you will.
He owes *NO ONE* an explanation for why He does
what He does, and why He allows what He allows.
He is God, and He is in control.

We are living in the last days,
and scripture is being fulfilled!

Things are happening fast, and remember, **God wants to use YOU!**
Be a vessel, be a blessing, be alert, be sober minded, be faithful,
be obedient, be merciful, be bold, be honest, and most important of all...
BE READY!

My Thoughts

63

'HE KNOWS THE END'

'I cry out, "My splendor is gone! Everything I had hoped for from the Lord is lost." The thought of my suffering and homelessness is bitter beyond words.
I will never forget this awful time, as I grieve over my loss.
Yet I still dare to hope when I remember this:
The faithful love of the Lord never ends!
His mercies never cease. (It is because of His mercies that we are not consumed.) Great is His faithfulness.
His mercies begin afresh each morning.'
-Lamentations 3:18-23

Sometimes things can get so out of control, and get so bad, that we begin to question the love of God! *'If you really love me Lord, WHY are you allowing all of this to happen to me?'*

Think about the many believers all over the world who have lost homes, jobs, loved ones, and how tragic their experiences must be.. Bring it closer to home. Think about some of the things you and your loved ones have faced over the last 12 months. Yet here in Lamentations, we see the transparency of the writer who says: YET I STILL DARE TO HOPE!!! That's it! Something on the inside of you can't give up! Although things may be bleak, and situations turn from bad to worse, you know that there is **HOPE in God!**

God's sovereignty cannot always be explained. It just is!

We will never fully understand that, and at some point we must come to grips with the fact that His ways are not our ways, and He has a much bigger plan in store.

All of the things that occur from day to day are shaping us into His image, and 'He knows' what we will look like in the end.

The process is hard, and we are constantly on the potter's wheel, yet He desires to get the best out of His investment!!!

He only wants us to trust Him...

Take hope in God! He is there.. and your challenge is only temporary! Remember, you are His investment!!!!!

My Thoughts

64

'Living Life on Purpose'

"Many are the plans in a man's heart, but it is the Lord's purpose that prevails."
-Proverbs 19:21

It is amazing how we grow up planning our lives.
We go to school, get a good education, get good jobs, marry, have kids, start our own businesses, retire, and watch our grandkids grow up...

That would be ideal.. but there's one factor missing...***GOD!***

His thoughts and ways are much different than ours.
We makes all these plans, and God says,
'Ok, looks good, but my plan looks different, so let's roll.'

You then find yourself on a journey where each day you are leaning, trusting, and depending on Him because you are unsure of what each day will bring!

Although this was not what you planned, you somehow find comfort and joy in knowing that your steps have been ordered, and your life is being governed by the One who knows exactly what's best for you!

God has a purpose and a plan for you that is much larger than you'll ever know! He is sovereign, and He knows and sees much more than we can!

Take rest in the fact that when you give Him the driver's seat of your life, you are in good hands, and you are living life on 'PURPOSE'!

My Thoughts

65

'How I Get Full'

"Then Jesus explained, "My nourishment comes from doing the will of God, who sent me, and from finishing His work."
-John 4:34

It is better to have a feeble beginning and a strong finish, than to have a strong beginning and no finish at all!

How you start matters, but how you end is more important.

I just want to remind you and encourage you today.. finish strong!

You may be at the point of letting go or giving up...but don't!
Finish what you've started! Things take time.. and you will get there.

There is a great reward waiting on the
other side of this journey you're enduring!

Take comfort in knowing that GOD gets
glory when you finish what you start!

Be patient, and focus on finishing!

My Thoughts

66

'My Thoughts are Different'

'For my thoughts are not your thoughts, neither are your ways my ways,' declares the Lord.
-Isaiah 55:8

The ways and thoughts of God are incomprehensible to man.

We can ask God 'WHY' all day long, but He cannot be demanded to give us an answer. He doesn't ever have to explain Himself.. He is God.

Although this may *'seem'* unfair, since we serve such a loving God, He desires that we TRUST Him, and believe that *'everything'* He does and allows in our lives is for our good, and is forming us into His image and likeness..

We may not **EVER** get the 'whys' to our questions answered in our lives, but as long as we know 'WHO' is in control brings more comfort and peace on a daily basis as we learn to trust the **WISDOM** of God!

This part is NOT a cake walk, and it is NOT easy, but God really does know what is best for us, and we have GOT to buckle down and believe that at some point.

Remember, just when you think, "Oh, I've finally figured it out! This happened so this could be like this, and this is what God is doing, and I know what's going to happen next, and I understand it all now..." Think again..

Those are YOUR thoughts and YOUR ways of human resolve, not His.

My Thoughts

67

'He Really Knows it All'

"I also withheld rain from you when the harvest was still three months away. I sent rain on one town, but withheld it from another. One field had rain, another had none and dried up."
-Amos 4:7

Many believe that there is no God, and that things just happen. Not true at all. Here we are reminded of God's sovereignty.

He causes the sun to shine, and the rain to fall. Whenever it rains, we are reminded that God is still in control and **'He knows'** exactly what we need.

'He knows' when to answer our prayers, and when to come through for His children. **'He knows'** what we need and what we 'don't' need.

'He knows' what to use as tools in our lives to bring out the best in us, and get us to the place of trusting in Him. **'He knows'**...*we don't*.

Our job is to trust Him, and believe that ALL things are working together for our good and for His glory. Hold on child of God.. **'HE KNOWS'**.

My Thoughts

68

'Covered and Protected'

*"But You Lord are a shield around me, my Glory,
the One who lifts my head up high."*
-Psalm 3:3

God is your protector. He is the One who covers you from dangers seen and unseen.

Don't lose your mind and get so upset
when unforeseen challenges and obstacles arise in your life.

It may just be that God is protecting you from things that
you have no clue 'could' be happening...
He sees what we can't see.. He knows what we don't know..
Remember, your steps are ordered!

If you're feeling low today, take courage in His word,
for He promises to lift your head up high again...
Things **WILL** get better!

You are covered, and you are protected.

My Thoughts

69

'Nothing is an Accident'

"When times are good, be happy; but when times are bad, consider: God has made the one as well as the other. Therefore a man cannot discover anything about his future."
-Ecclesiastes 7:14

Everything in your life happens for a God-given reason.
Nothing is an accident, and the devil is NOT to be blamed!

God is in complete control of it ALL!

God has not looked the other way, or been caught by
surprise when adversity strikes us.

He is in control of that adversity, directing it for His glory,
and for our good! He allows it all!

Think about it, we often make our plans,
but are forced somehow to change those plans.

We must always keep in mind: our 'unexpected' forced change of plans,
is a part of His plan!

Take one day at a time, step by step,
moving forward, and trusting Him!

My Thoughts

70

'Maximum Glory'

"Who can speak and have it happen if the Lord has not decreed it?"
-Lamentations 3:37

God is sovereign. He is in control of everything that happens in your life...everything.

Nothing can happen to you that He hasn't purposed to be part of the bigger picture for the plan and purpose for your life.

Yes, sometimes that may be difficult to hear or understand, but He is a loving Father that is not out to harm you, but to bring about His will in the earth, and to get the maximum glory out of your life.

Continue to stand strong, and trust Him no matter what! He is in control.

Once this is over, you will understand that God always looks at the bigger picture. You get the growth, He gets the Glory!

My Thoughts

71

'Don't be Scared'

"Fear not [there is nothing to fear], for I am with you...I will help you; yes, I will hold you up and retain you with My [victorious] right hand..."
-Isaiah 41:10 (AMP)

We all face times in life that feel out of our control.

In the tough times, it's easy to get discouraged and allow fear to creep in; but instead, why not focus on the fact that God is holding you in the palm of His hand!

Nothing is too difficult for God; and nothing is beyond His ability. He is our Father, and will graciously see us through the storm.

When God holds us, we are safe; and our security is guaranteed! In His hand, there is victory, strength, power, provision, and ALL that we need!

No matter what you may be going through today, you can trust that God is for you.

Instead of giving up and getting depressed over our circumstances, we need to look up and see GOD! As we keep our hearts and minds focused on Him, we will see Him move in ways beyond what our minds could ever imagine!

Remember, when you don't have the strength to hold yourself up, His hand is there... and HE will!

Don't fear! He's got you IN HIS HANDS!!!!!!!

My Thoughts

72

'Don't Forget to Dream'

'And Joseph dreamed a dream, and he told it to his brethren, and they hated him yet the more.'
-Genesis 37:5

Dare to dream.. dream again with no excuses!
There will be people all around you who will be like Joseph's brothers, ...but keep dreaming!

Dream big! Aim for the sky! I admit wholeheartedly, It can be difficult to dream when your dreams take so long to come to pass, but don't stop dreaming!

It can also be difficult to dream when you have little or no support from those who you believe should be encouraging your dreams.

However, don't let that shake you.. stop 'expecting others', and 'EXPECT GOD'!

Remember, it was 30 years or more until Joseph saw his dreams manifest! In between the dream and his promise, he was hated on, sold into slavery, lied on, forgotten, thrown into prison, yet the bible says: 'And the Lord was with Joseph'!

It takes a determined faith and trust in God to keep the dream in your heart alive! ..and remember, it's ALL about God's timing! Your duty is to DREAM!

DREAM.. no matter what.. and watch God move..

My Thoughts

73

'Keep it Up'

"The things that you have learned, and received, and heard, and seen in me, do those things, and the God of peace shall be with you."
-Philippians 4:9

God gives us great opportunity each year to learn valuable lessons. Many situations are placed in front of us to see how we will handle them, and allow ourselves to see exactly what we are made of.

Reflecting back on this year, have you learned anything? Have you seen God come through for you? Are you stronger? Have you grow spiritually?

As you go through life, don't forget to take all of the valuable things you've learned along with you. Sometimes we tend to forget how far God has brought us and the things He has brought us through! Let's not allow that to be true for us any longer...

I encourage you as you move forward each day, to keep up the good work! Keep praising God! Keep reminding yourself of His faithfulness! Keep pressing in! Keep forgiving! Keep trusting! Keep loving! Keep seeing yourself and others through His eyes! ...and above all.. Keep the faith!

My Thoughts

74

'What's Your Name?'

"A good name is rather to be chosen than great riches.."
-Proverbs 22:1

Think about this.. when you hear the name of certain people,
what is the feeling or emotion that comes to mind?

You want to be the kind of person that always makes a difference..

Do you add to people's lives that are around you, or do you subtract?
Do you positively multiply to the people's lives you're in, or do you divide?

Do you complicate their lives, or help simplify?
After a visit with you, do they leave more at peace, or are they more confused?

Do you inspire them to be better, happier, more disciplined?

What do people think of when they hear 'your' name?

My Thoughts

75

'Never Stop Praying'

"Pray without ceasing.."
-1 Thessalonians 5:16

Never stop praying..
When things are good.. pray,
When things aren't so good...pray,
When in doubt and worry...pray,
When in need...pray,
When you're grateful...pray,
When you're confused.. pray
When you feel alone...pray,
When you're afraid...pray,
When you get it right...pray,
When you blow it...pray,

Pray, pray, pray...

Whatever state you find yourself in...pray..

Talk to your Father... He loves it when you communicate with Him!

Never stop praying...

My Thoughts

76

'STAY IN THE FIGHT'

'You then, my son, be strong in the grace that is in Christ Jesus...
Endure hardship with us like a good soldier of Christ Jesus.'
-2 Timothy 2: 1,3 (NIV)

When you gave your life to Christ, you entered into a spiritual battle
that will last you for the rest of your life.

There will be many victories while fighting this battle,
and there will also be casualties along the way.

Our job as believers is to stay in the fight, and continue moving forward,
knowing that God is fighting for us and with us.

It's about sticking with Him when the clouds are blue,
and even when the skies are filled with dark clouds.

Through thick and thin, through every heartache and trial, we must continue to stand, fight, trust God, and move forward!

We must endure... it is what we are called to do!

My Thoughts

77

'Following Directions'

"Trust in the Lord, and lean not on your own understanding, In all you do, acknowledge God first, and He will give you direction.."
-Proverbs 3:5,6

Don't ever think that little things don't matter to God. Everything matters.. He says to acknowledge Him in ALL you do..

That means communicate, ask questions, seek His counsel.. BEFORE making a decision, and HE will direct you the way that you should go.

It would save us a lot of time and trouble if we would just learn to ask God first!

He says: 'Don't lean or depend on the way YOU think the pieces should fit, ask ME first!'

He knows what we don't know, He sees what we can't see, and He has ALL of the answers to our questions..

Trust God, and seek Him first about **EVERYTHING**! It **ALL** matters to Him...

My Thoughts

78

'Knock, Knock'

*"God is a safe house for the battered, a sanctuary during bad times.
The moment you arrive, you relax; you're never sorry you knocked."*
-Psalm 8:9-10 (Message)

Run to God! There, and only there is assured safety!
He will cover you in the bad times, and lighten your load.

Getting into the presence of God will calm you down, and bring peace to your heart.

You may not get every answer to your questions, but He will give you peace.

Why not try Him first, rather than spin your wheels going in circles...
If you're feeling a little beat-up or battered, try knocking on God's door for a change..

TRY GOD...GOD CAN!

My Thoughts

79

'WEIGHTLIFTING 101'

"For our light affliction, which is but for a moment, is working for us a far more exceeding and eternal weight of glory."
-2 Corinthians 4:17

Our affliction, whether great or small, is only for a little while. It will make us stronger and will cause us to grow closer to Christ.

Although we may not understand it, and although the pain may feel unbearable, our promise as believers is that one day we will see Jesus face to face, and it will all be worth it.

No matter what you're going through, keep the goal in mind. His promises are true.

It will get tough, and the road may twist a bit, but the Glory that will be revealed in the end will outweigh your darkest days. It's all a part of the journey!

Buckle up, hold on, and ride with God...

My Thoughts

80

'Yes You Can'

"I can do ALL things through Christ as He gives me more and more strength!'
-Philippians 4:13

Yes you can!
Don't quit! Don't give up!

Again..
Yes you can!
Don't quit! Don't give up!

Focus on the goal.. and not on where you are..
this is temporary..
Trust the process...

Although you're in this place, you've trusted the process before, and you came through..

Don't forget to remember!

Don't quit now! Keep moving forward!!!
Yes you can...

My Thoughts

81

'LIPS THAT HEAL'

"Kind words heal and help; cutting words wound and maim."
-Proverbs 15:4

Be careful and mindful of what you say to people.
Everyone could use an encouraging word.

Life is challenging on every hand, and you may be the very one who can lift a person's spirit in their time of need.

It doesn't make you weak to be nice. It doesn't take anything away from you to hold back a negative comment, and to give an encouraging word.

What it does, is opens an opportunity for God to use you to be a blessing to someone else.

Be 'selfless', not selfish.. watch what you let come out of your mouth..

My Thoughts

82

'No Time to Waste Time'

"Teach us to realize the brevity of life, so that we may grow in wisdom."
-Psalms 90:12

Make sure you use your time wisely... Don't spend time worrying about things that you have no control over.

Life is much too precious to major in the minors...

Don't spend extra time trying to help others who don't want to be helped...

Learn from your mistakes, and keep moving forward!

Realize that to someone, you are the best thing since sliced bread, and they want, need, and will take heed to your advice!

Live with no regrets., and simply make better choices!

You don't have time to waste time!

Enjoy the journey..

My Thoughts

83

'IN THE RIGHT DIRECTION'

"Look straight ahead, and fix your eyes on what lies before you.."
-Proverbs 4:25

Stop being distracted by the past! It was what it was, and God's grace has carried you through. You are exactly where you are supposed to be.. and yes, your steps have been ordered...

It was all allowed to teach you more about God's unconditional love, and bring you closer to Him.

You haven't missed a thing, and what God has for you- no one else can take! Stay focused on your goals, and stay in your lane!

Take a little time to revisit your dreams and goals!
What has He told you to do that you still haven't followed through with?

In this life, there will always be 'things' for you to do,
but it's time to 'do the things' He's told you to do!
It's never too late, and He's provided you with
everything you need to get started!

'Be the change you'd like to see!' Stop waiting, and DO something..

My Thoughts

84

'If I Can Do it, You Can Too'

*"Imitate God, in everything you do, because
you are His dear children.
Live a life filled with love, following the example of Christ."*
-Ephesians 5:1-2

We've all heard the phrase: 'When I move, you move, just like that.'
This is what God says to us today.
He says: 'Imitate my love.. If I can forgive, so should you..
If I can bless instead of curse, so should you..
If I can see the potential others have, and believe the best,
instead of how they may choose to act right now, so should you..'

We have a great example in Christ Jesus,
and He says to us today: "If I can do it, you can too..
You can do anything, and nothing is impossible,
especially if you do it in MY strength, and not your own..
Follow my lead, and imitate Me. When I move, you move... just like that!"

My Thoughts

85

'HIS LOVE NEVER FAILS'

'It is better to trust in the Lord, than to put confidence in man.'
-Psalms 118:8

Save yourself the heartache, disappointment, stress, blame, and anger..
of putting your trust elsewhere..

Take hold of this simple admonishment and walk in it!

Trust God.. He knows (better than anyone else) how to deal with your tender heart..
...and He loves you beyond what you could ever imagine..

Are you getting it yet? Put your trust in Him!

His love.. God's love.. NEVER fails!

My Thoughts

86

'A Change of Plans'

'A man's mind plans his way, but the Lord directs his steps and makes them sure.'
-Proverbs 16:9 (AMP)

Many times we go through life making lots of plans,
having dreams in our hearts that we've carried since we were little kids.
It is great to dream, and very important to plan, but remember,
God orders our steps..

When things don't happen the way you've planned or expected them to, don't lose heart.. God knows what is best for you, and although you may not understand why the things you've worked so hard at getting accomplished haven't taken you further, trust God, and know that His plan for your life is SURE.

Don't fight it, let go and let God!
You are right where you are meant to be!

Say this prayer with me:
Dear Lord, I have made many plans for my life, and I have many dreams in my heart.
I place those plans and dreams in Your hand, and ask You to have Your way in my life. I surrender, and I trust You Lord. In the name of Jesus, Amen

My Thoughts

87

'Conditions Change'

'To everything there is a season, and a time for every matter or purpose under heaven.'
-Ecclesiastes 3:1

Conditions change all the time. What you could depend on yesterday, might very well be gone today.

What once worked so well for you, will eventually fail to bring the results you seek. So when conditions change, you have the valuable opportunity to change along with them.

Life, by its very definition, is always changing. People who make the most of life are those who expect the changes, welcome them, and find the positive possibilities in each one.

When you see changes occurring, instead of making a judgment, make a careful observation. You cannot stop the changes that are already taking place, so your best strategy is to find the opportunities that are embedded within them.

Rather than being fearful of the changes, embrace them.

You can count on the fact that the world will continue to change. The sooner you accept it, the better off you'll be.

My Thoughts

88

'WE HAVE HELP'

"..and the Holy Spirit helps us in our weakness, for when we do not know what to pray, the Holy Spirit prays for us with groanings that cannot be expressed in words."
-Romans 8:26

Even when we don't know what to pray, God is still moving.
When we don't have the strength to pray, God is strong
on our behalf.

As believers, we will experience moments in
this life that will leave us speechless.... yet there is help.

It is in those times that God says:
"Be still, and know that I am God.
I will come to your rescue."

Keep trusting Him, He will carry you through.. HE will help you..

He will pray for you..

My Thoughts

89

'Say What You Need to Say'

'It's not what goes into your mouth that defiles you; you are defiled by the words that come out of your mouth.'
-Matthew 15:11

Watch what you say.
Think (a few times) before you open your mouth.
Listen first, and then speak.

Don't assume, and don't speculate.
Use your words to uplift another.
As much as possible, be positive.
Let your words encourage another's life today.

Speak life over your OWN life today..
Speak life into your OWN situation..

You have the power to change the atmosphere around you with your words!
Don't wait for someone else to encourage you.. say what YOU need to say..

Don't pass up the opportunity to speak into another person's life today.
Don't be thrown off by their facial expressions or their body language..
The very ones that you think don't need it,
are usually the ones who need it the most!

My Thoughts

90

'Extra-Ordinary'

'Good planning and hard work lead to prosperity, but hasty shortcuts lead to poverty.'
-Proverbs 21:5

Whatever you do, do it with all of your heart.
Shortcuts may seem to get you to your destination faster,
but may not profit you in the end...

Be more organized.. take time to plan..
Think things through..

It's been said before:
One who fails to plan, plans to fail..
Also, the only difference between the word
ordinary and extraordinary is the word 'extra'..

In order to have more than what you or others already have,
you've got to do more than what you and others have been willing to do...

Do the extra... it matters!

My Thoughts

91

'DON'T JUMP TO CONCLUSIONS'

'He that answers a matter before he hears it, it is folly and shame unto him..'
-Proverbs 18:13

Learn to be a good listener. Don't just assume that you know. Try asking more questions and gathering more facts before commenting, or offering your advice on a matter.

You may feel that you've seen this a million times, and this is no different from the last time you heard something like this....

Remember that everyone's situation is different, and many times there is much more to a story than the obvious..

Before jumping to conclusions and being so quick to offer your help and a solution, take a second to listen a little bit longer..

There is great wisdom in learning to listen.

My Thoughts

92

'GET THE VISINE'

"..and why do you behold the mote that is in thy brother's eye, but perceivest not the beam that is in thine own eye?"
-Luke 6:41

Check yourself. Stop looking around and finding so much
to say about others. Spend more time focusing on your goals,
your dreams, your family, your finances, your plans, your situation...
and becoming a better you!

Everyone has issues. We all have sinned and
continue to fall short of God's glory.. daily!

Why is it that we feel we can help solve everyone else's problems,
but have no resolve when it comes to dealing with our own stuff..?

Don't be the judge. If you have nothing positive to say,
keep quiet, keep it moving, and just pray!

If anything, be the shoulder that someone may need to lean on.

My Thoughts

93

'It's Already Worked Out'

"Be still and know that I am GOD!"..
I will be exalted among the heathen,
I will be exalted in the earth..
-Psalms 46:10

Trust God! He will provide for every one of your needs.

Don't frustrate yourself about the why's of life.. keep your eyes on God! You've got to 'KNOW' that if He allows it, it's a set up for what's next...

Don't blame anyone else, hold your tongue, and focus!
With Him, there's ALWAYS a bigger picture..

Remember how many generations came and went before the birth of our Savior..?
Many kings ruled, but ultimately would set up the grand entrance for the King of Kings to step onto the scene..

Just know that your blessing is tied to someone else's, and that God is always up to great things concerning you!

His plan for all of us is good... we just have to learn to be patient, waiting and trusting that in His time, things will come together.

Until then, be still, and know your God..

My Thoughts

94

'IT'S BOUND TO HAPPEN'

"Here on earth you will have many trials and sorrows; but take heart, I have overcome the world."
-John 16:33

"Because He lives, I can face tomorrow".. That's a line to an old spiritual song that's been around for decades.

For the believer, this song comes to life at many points along the way in our lives. Being a follower of Christ doesn't give us a 'problem free life pass'!

In this life, we will face many challenges and obstacles. It doesn't matter where you were born, who your parents are, or what type of education you have, you will face *many* challenges. No one is exempt from the trials and tribulations of this life.

Yet, Jesus tells us to take heart, knowing that He has overcome the world. When this life is over, we will see Him face to face, and finally meet the One who gave His very life for us, so that once we pass through our earthly journey, we can spend eternity with Him.. problem free, worry free, stress free, fear free, trouble free, pain free, hurt free, disease free, and so much more..

Can you imagine that? Knowing this dims the light on some of the issues that seem to shine so bright when we put it all into perspective!

Although we may not like it, God Himself assures us that we WILL have MANY trials and sorrows in this life, so we shouldn't be surprised when they come!

One day, it will be over.. TAKE HEART!

My Thoughts

95

'A Greater Love'

"For great is Your love, higher than the heavens."
-Psalm 108:4 (NIV)

The love of the Lord is indescribable at times..

He takes the broken hearted, and mends every piece.
He takes the rejected and abandoned, and showers His acceptance and favor upon them.

It never matters how far you've strayed, or how long you've strayed, God's arms are always stretched out and ready to receive the weary soul.

It is funny how the human mind thinks. When we are hurt or intentionally mistreated, we seek revenge and justification. We will even go as far to try and hurt the one who has hurt us even more than what they did to us.

Not so with the Father. We disobey daily, and yet He says "Come, I forgive you and I love you."

We walk away from assignments that we 'feel' we can't handle, and He says "It's ok, get back up and try again, I am with you."

My Thoughts

96

'Live Life on Purpose'

"Set your affection on things above, not on things on the earth."
-Colossians 3:2

Everything that we experience on earth is but for a moment.

All of our successes, and victories are but for a moment. The hurt, the disappointment, the tears, the loss, the suffering, the sickness... all of it is but for a moment in time.

Don't get so attached to earthly possessions or experiences. Cherish them, rejoice for them, enjoy them, but don't build a house there.. rather pitch a tent.

All things on earth are temporary and subject to change. God gives us things to embrace and enjoy while we are here, occupying time until His return.

The friendships, relationships, our jobs, careers, and even our families will only be able to be shared on earth for a season...

That's why it is so important to spend every moment 'on purpose'! Tell those people that you care about how much they mean to you. Enjoy precious moments, and special moments, and take it all in...

One day, things will change, and when they do, you want to be in a place with God that says: 'Thank you Lord for allowing me to have that experience...' Now let Your will be done in Jesus' name...

Live life 'on purpose'.

My Thoughts

97

'WHY IS THIS HAPPENING?'

*"My brethren, count it all joy when trouble comes your way;
knowing this, that the testing of your faith produces endurance."*
-James 1:2-3

What you are enduring right now is for your good! I know it doesn't 'feel' good, but it's going to work out for the good.

It is developing your spiritual muscles. It's working patience in you for the journey.

Think of how far you've come. The things that used to get to you don't get to you as much now. The things that used to worry you all night and stay on your mind all day seem to dissipate quicker now...

Now that you are spending time with God, you understand that when He allows something to come into your life, it is there on purpose, and that He has a plan for it.

You've even been able to help others understand it, because you've been through it.

Continue to give thanks and rejoice that once you come out of this, (just like He brought you out last time) you're going to be even better, and that you are developing patience.

My Thoughts

98

'The Work is Finished'

"There is therefore now no condemnation to them which are in Christ Jesus, who walk not after the flesh, but after the Spirit."
-Romans 8:1

The law of the Spirit of life in Christ Jesus has made us free from the law of sin and death.

That does NOT mean that we are to live any kind of life that we want to causing the Grace of God to be cheapened.

There are many who say: 'Oh now that Christ has paid for all of my sins past, present, and future, I can do my thing and He will forgive me!' That is deception from the enemy, and is a mockery of the cross!

For the believer in Christ, yes Jesus did die for all of the sins that we have committed, and for every one that we will commit. In contrast, that should not at all make us to believe that we have a license to live any kind of way. It should rather bring us to our knees, and to tears to see and experience this great sacrifice and great love!

It should cause us to DESIRE to live for Him even more, and give of ourselves freely to others!

What an amazing gift of love, that He would give to you and I...

What a loving Father we have..

My Thoughts

99

'He Controls it with His Hands'

"The king's heart is in the hand of the Lord, as the rivers of water, He turns it whichever way He wants."
-Proverbs 21: 1

The battle is the Lord's! Again.. the battle is the Lord's!

It doesn't matter what they are trying to do to you, or the accusations they've thrown your way.. in the end, you will win!

Pray that God will turn their hearts in your favor...

Their hearts may be hardened even harder than Pharaoh's, but the king's hearts are in His hands and He has the power to turn them whichever way He pleases!

If He is allowing it to be this way for now, trust His plan...

If you don't understand, and you are still wrestling.. trust His heart!

His intentions for you are good!

When it's time, HE will turn it for your good, and for His glory!

My Thoughts

100

'Renewed Strength'

"Your strength shall be renewed day by day like morning dew."
-Psalm 110:3 (TLB)

Today you woke up with brand new mercies..

Today is a day that you have never seen before. Yesterday is a memory of the past, and there is absolutely nothing that you can change that happened yesterday.

There are people waiting for the exchange of words that you will have with them today.

Make sure you add to their lives. Make sure to say something uplifting, and encouraging. Don't let them leave your presence the same way they were once they encountered you today.

Be God's hands, feet, and lips today..

You have a fresh start today to get things done that you may have left undone yesterday.

Take advantage of this moment, and make it a good one..

You have everything you need for this day to happen! You are prepared.. Go make history!

My Thoughts

About the Author

Kurt Lykes is a published songwriter and author, and is currently the Minister of Music at The Center of Hope (First Church of God) in Inglewood, Ca. Kurt leads worship throughout the nation, his primary gift being one that equips and develops the Body of Christ in the area of worship.

Kurt expresses his love and passion for his inspirational devotionals and songwriting by saying, *"What comes from the heart reaches the heart, and I believe what people are searching for is something they can relate to. I believe my gift has been given to capture that reader and / or listener, and their heart, so that they can experience and prayerfully begin to understand God's captivating love."*

Made in United States
Orlando, FL
15 October 2023